C000245946

ELECTRICITY

Let's Investigate

by Ruth Owen and Victoria Dobney

Consultant:

Nicky Waller

RubY TuesdAY BOOKS

Published in 2019 by Ruby Tuesday Books Ltd.

Copyright © 2019 Ruby Tuesday Books Ltd.

All rights reserved. No part of this publication may be reproduced in whole or in part, stored in any retrieval system, or transmitted in any form or by any means, electronic, mechanical, photocopying, recording, or otherwise, without written permission from the publisher.

Editor: Mark J. Sachner
Designers: Emma Randall and Tammy West
Production: John Lingham

Photo credits:
Alamy: 26 (left), 27 (top); Creative Commons: 19 (bottom), 28 (bottom); NASA: 4 (bottom); Ruby Tuesday Books: 14—15, 17; Science Photo Library: 20 (top); Shutterstock: Cover, 1, 2—3, 4—5, 6—7, 8—9, 10—11, 12 (top), 13, 16, 18, 19 (top), 20 (bottom), 21, 23, 24—25, 26 (right), 27 (bottom), 28 (top), 29; Superstock: 12 (bottom), 22.

ISBN 978-1-78856-043-6

Printed in China by Toppan Leefung Printing Limited

www.rubytuesdaybooks.com

Contents

The download button shows there are free
worksheets or other resources available.
Go to:
www.rubytuesdaybooks.com/scienceKS2

Switched ON

Here's a BIG challenge. Can you think of something you've done today that didn't require electricity?

You might say "eating a bowl of cereal". But the cereal was produced and packaged in a factory by machines that use electricity.

Maybe you said "walking to school". But unless you were barefoot, your shoes were made in a factory and the road or pavement was built using electrically powered tools and machines.

energy

It's a pretty difficult challenge, isn't it?

Electricity is a form of **energy** that is used in thousands of different ways. And today, in many countries around the world, it touches almost every part of our lives.

Let's Investigate

Look carefully at each of the pictures and describe what you observe.

Which of the objects do you think are powered by electricity?

Lawnmower

Phone

Barbecue

Digital alarm clock

Garden light with solar panel

Kettle

Toothbrush

Vacuum cleaner

Alarm clock

Washing machine

(The answers are on page 32.)

What Is Electricity?

You can't see electricity, but when you switch on your laptop or a lamp, you know it's there supplying power. So what exactly is electricity?

Everything is made from tiny **atoms**, which contain even smaller **particles** called **electrons**. When electrons flow along wires, this creates electricity, or an **electric current**.

If you could see the flow of electrons inside a wire, they might look something like this.

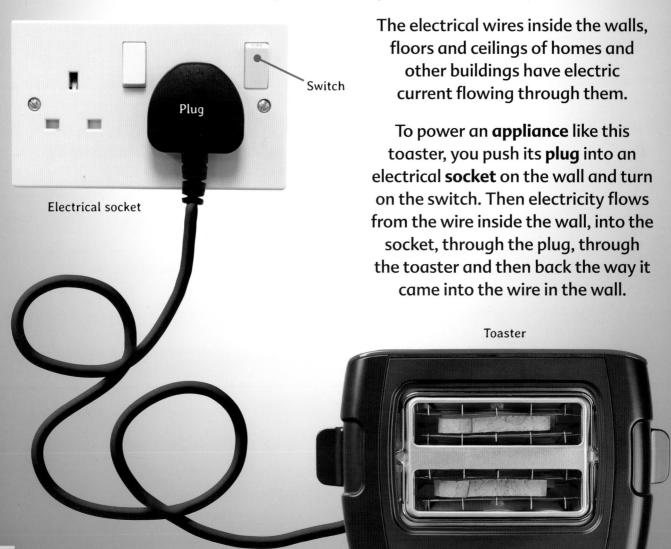

Switch

Plug

Electrical socket

The electrical wires inside the walls, floors and ceilings of homes and other buildings have electric current flowing through them.

To power an **appliance** like this toaster, you push its **plug** into an electrical **socket** on the wall and turn on the switch. Then electricity flows from the wire inside the wall, into the socket, through the plug, through the toaster and then back the way it came into the wire in the wall.

Toaster

UK plug

Plugs come in different designs around the world.

US plug

European plug

This electrician is installing electrical wiring inside the walls of a new house.

DANGER

Electricity is an everyday part of our lives. But it can be highly dangerous, causing serious injuries and even death. Always follow these important safety rules.

- NEVER go near or play near **substations**, **pylons** or any other buildings or equipment belonging to **power stations** or electricity suppliers.

- Keep watch for electrical cables when climbing trees or flying kites. Electricity from the cable could flow straight down the kite string and through your body. Make sure adults are careful, too, when using ladders that might touch a cable.

- Keep all electrical items away from water. Electricity can flow through water and into your body.

- Never poke anything into electrical sockets. They are for plugs only!

- Never dismantle electrical devices or appliances – even if they are unplugged. If you want to know how something works, go online and watch an informative YouTube video.

- Don't overload electrical sockets or extension cords as they may catch fire.

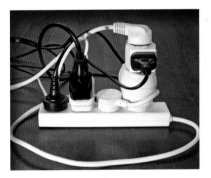

- Always unplug by holding the actual plug, not by pulling on the wire. You can damage the appliance, the plug or the socket.

What Is a Battery?

The kind of electricity that flows through the wires in our homes is **mains electricity**. It can only be used by connecting electrical items to the wires carrying the electricity. A **battery** makes electrical energy inside your phone, tablet or torch — and it can go anywhere.

Depending on the size and type of battery, the power may last for hours, days, weeks or even years.

Inside a Battery

A battery has an outer casing made of plastic or metal.

It also has two metal terminals on the outside marked with a plus (+) and a minus (–) symbol.

Inside the battery are chemicals.

The battery in the **circuit** below has been connected to a bulb.

A wire runs from the negative, or minus (–), terminal, through the bulb and back to the positive, or plus (+), terminal.

When everything is connected, a **chemical reaction** takes place inside the battery which creates a flow of electrical energy.

Just like the wires in your home, the reaction causes electrons to flow through the wire from the minus terminal to the plus terminal.

The electric current they produce lights up the bulb.

Eventually, the chemical reaction stops happening, the battery dies and it can no longer be used.

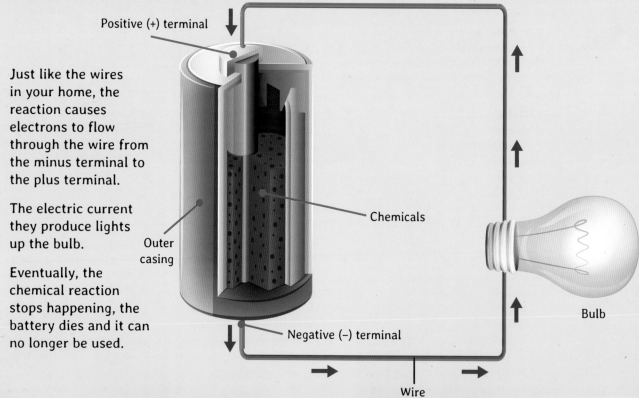

Positive (+) terminal

Chemicals

Outer casing

Negative (–) terminal

Bulb

Wire

Batteries come in many shapes and sizes, allowing us to power differently sized electrical items. The packaging of a new electrical item will tell you what size battery it uses.

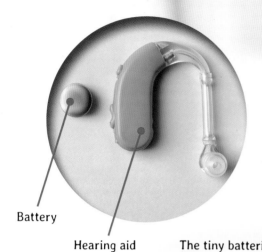

Battery

Hearing aid

Hearing aid

The tiny batteries that power a hearing aid are smaller than your little fingernail.

A battery dies when it has given out all its energy and is discharged.

Some batteries, however, can be recharged by plugging them into mains electricity using a charger.

As mains electricity runs through the battery, the chemicals inside reset and go back to how they were before the battery discharged.

The newly stored energy allows the chemical reactions to start up and the battery can once again be used to power electrical items.

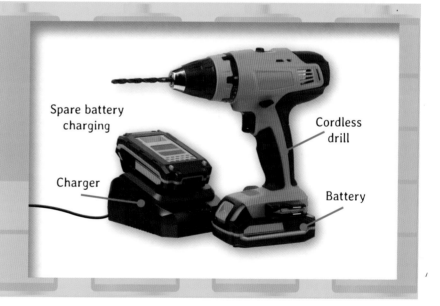

Spare battery charging

Cordless drill

Charger

Battery

Cells and Batteries

When we're talking about batteries in everyday life, we call a battery a "battery". But in scientific language, a single battery is actually called a **cell**. When two or more cells are used together to power a circuit, then they are known as a battery.

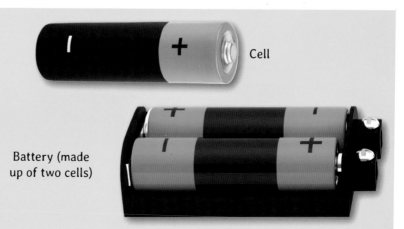

Cell

Battery (made up of two cells)

All About Circuits

In order for electricity to power an item, it must travel around a circuit. A circuit is a little like a running track that the electrons flow around and around in one direction, producing an electric current.

A simple circuit to switch a bulb on and off is made up of four **components**.

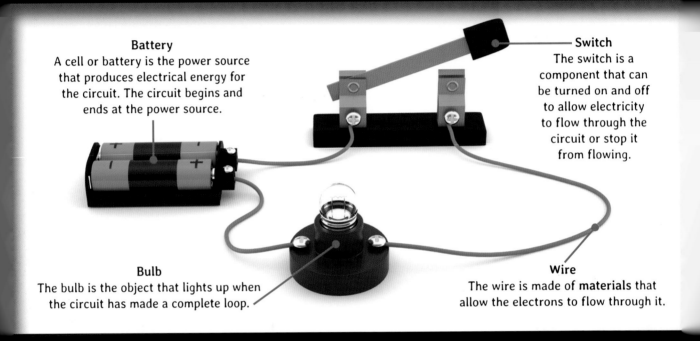

Battery
A cell or battery is the power source that produces electrical energy for the circuit. The circuit begins and ends at the power source.

Switch
The switch is a component that can be turned on and off to allow electricity to flow through the circuit or stop it from flowing.

Bulb
The bulb is the object that lights up when the circuit has made a complete loop.

Wire
The wire is made of **materials** that allow the electrons to flow through it.

Drawing Circuits

When we draw electrical circuits, we use symbols to show the different components of the circuit. A circuit might make a bulb light up or make a buzzer buzz.

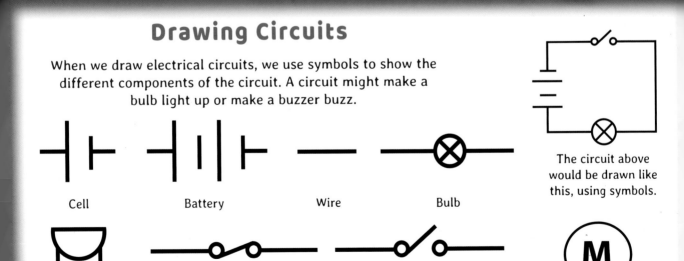

Cell

Battery

Wire

Bulb

The circuit above would be drawn like this, using symbols.

Buzzer

Switch on (closed)

Switch off (open)

Motor

Switches: On and Off

A switch is connected to a circuit by the wire and allows the flow of electricity around the circuit. You can think of a switch as a bridge connecting two halves of a road together. When the bridge is down, it allows cars to cross over. When the bridge is up, cars can't cross. When a switch is on or closed (down), electricity can cross and continue around the circuit. When the switch is off or open (up) the electricity can't reach the other side.

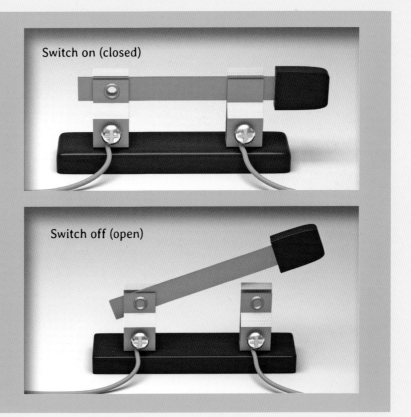

Switch on (closed)

Switch off (open)

A Circuit in Action

Any electrical item or device that runs on batteries has a circuit inside. They may look different from the circuits on these pages, but they work in exactly the same way.

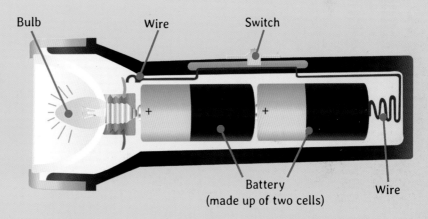

Bulb   Wire   Switch

Battery
(made up of two cells)

Wire

Your Home's Circuit

Electrical current must always flow in a circuit. You can think of a circuit as a circle or never-ending loop. Electricity flows from the power station where it is produced, along thick cables into your home, around the wires in your home, into your devices and other appliances and then back to the power station again. This is called a closed circuit.

Conductors and Insulators

Electricity cannot flow through all materials.

The materials that let an electrical current flow through them easily are called **conductors**. Materials that stop electricity flowing are called **insulators**. Let's investigate!

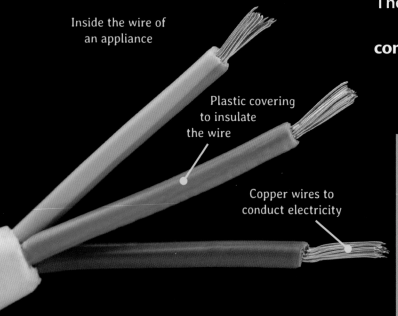

Inside the wire of an appliance

Plastic covering to insulate the wire

Copper wires to conduct electricity

Metals such as copper, iron and steel are good conductors of electricity. The wires that carry electricity around our homes are made of copper.

Materials such as plastic, rubber and wood are insulators. These materials do not allow electricity to pass through them.

Wires and plugs are covered with plastic to stop people or animals getting an electric shock from the electricity flowing through them.

Inside a UK Plug

The brown LIVE wire carries the electricity that's come all the way from the power station.

The blue NEUTRAL wire carries the electricity back into the circuit once it has passed through the appliance.

The striped EARTH wire is there for safety. If something goes wrong in the plug, it helps stop the appliance giving you an electric shock.

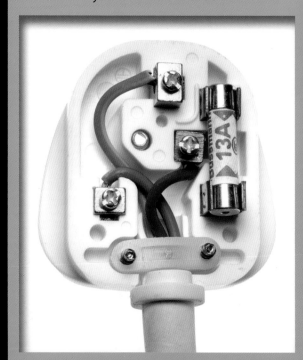

Let's Investigate

Conductor or Insulator?

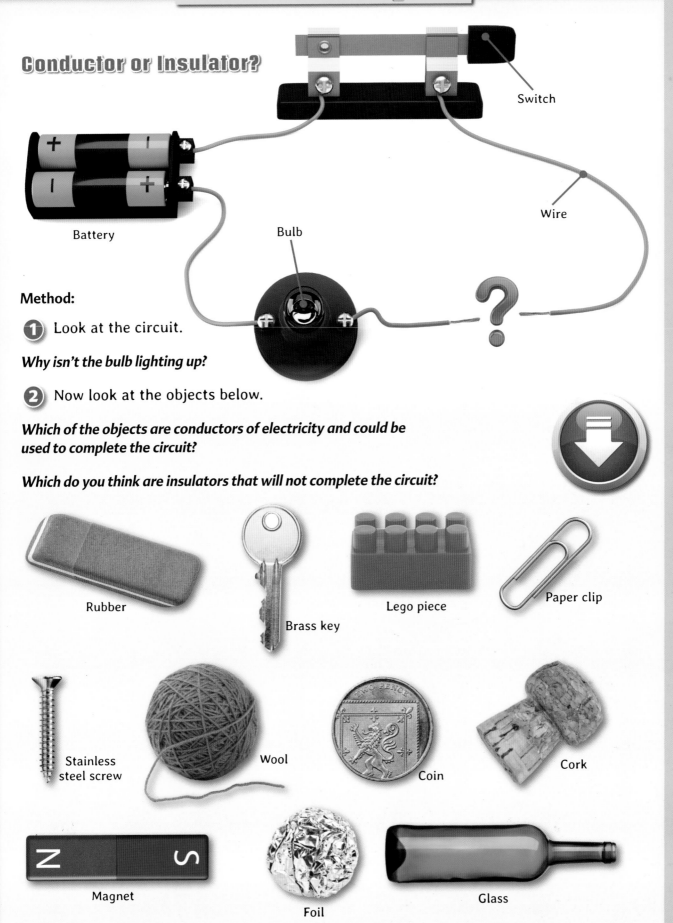

Switch

Wire

Battery

Bulb

Method:

1 Look at the circuit.

Why isn't the bulb lighting up?

2 Now look at the objects below.

Which of the objects are conductors of electricity and could be used to complete the circuit?

Which do you think are insulators that will not complete the circuit?

Rubber

Brass key

Lego piece

Paper clip

Stainless steel screw

Wool

Coin

Cork

Magnet

Foil

Glass

Working with Circuits

Circuits can be made up in many different ways. But in order for the electricity to keep flowing, a circuit must not be broken.

The flow of electricity in a circuit is called the current. The amount of pressure pushing the current around a circuit is the **voltage**.

The components in a circuit don't always look the same.

These are the components from an electrical kit that we're going to use to make some circuits.

Cell

Switch

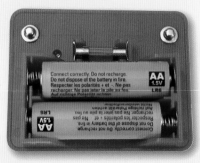

Battery (two cells)

Bulb

Wires (inside connector strips)

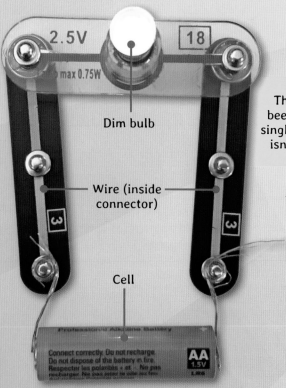

Dim bulb

Wire (inside connector)

Cell

The cell has been connected up to the circuit using copper wire.

This circuit has been made with a single cell. The bulb isn't very bright.

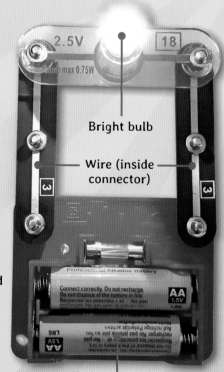

Bright bulb

Wire (inside connector)

The bulb in this circuit is very bright. That's because it's powered by a battery made of two cells that's producing twice the amount of voltage as a single cell.

Battery made of two cells

Voltage is measured with a unit of measurement called a **volt**. The number of volts on a cell (or battery) tells us how much it will push the current. More volts means more power.

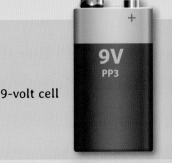 

9-volt cell

1.5-volt cell

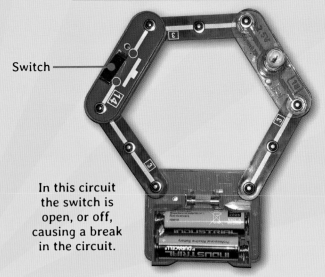

Switch

In this circuit the switch is open, or off, causing a break in the circuit.

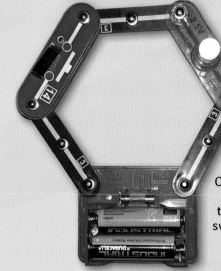

Once the break is closed by turning on the switch, the bulb lights up.

Series and Parallel Circuits

In a series circuit, the electricity can only move around one route. If a wire is disconnected or a component breaks, the circuit stops working.

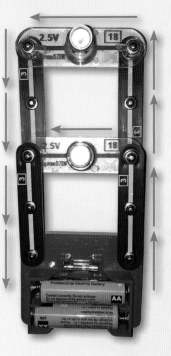

In a parallel circuit, the electricity has more than one route that it can take to flow from the battery and back again.

This parallel circuit is lighting two bulbs.

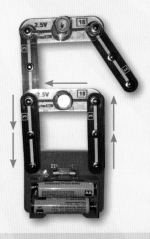

This parallel circuit has broken, but there is still a loop for the electricity to follow back to the battery.

In this broken parallel circuit, the electricity cannot flow in a loop back to the battery.

Let's Revise It!

So far we've discovered a lot about how electricity works.
How much can you remember? Let's revise it!

Make a Circuit

Choose four objects that when connected will make a circuit that can conduct electricity and light up a bulb. Why did you choose your four objects?

Plastic-covered copper wire

Rubber duck

Paper clip

Marble

Bulb

Magnet

Twig

Cell

Choose four objects that will make a circuit that won't light up a bulb. Explain your answer.

Matching Symbols

3

4

Try pairing up the pictures with the symbols that match them.

ON
OFF

A

B

C

2

G

ON
OFF

F

1

5

D

E

6

7

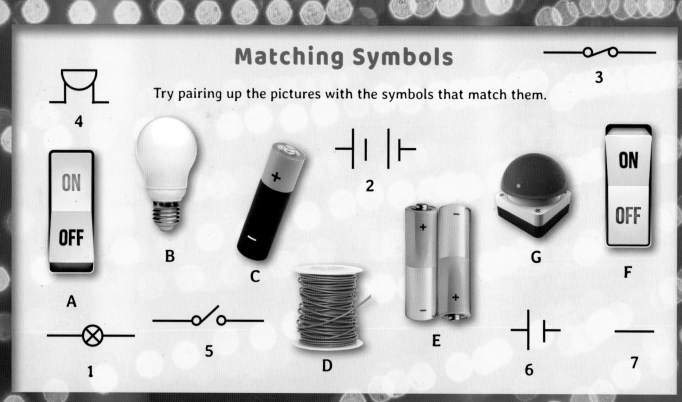

16

Make the Connection

Observe these diagrams of electrical circuits and try to answer the questions.

Circuit 1
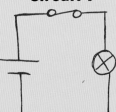

What four components make up this circuit?

Circuit 2
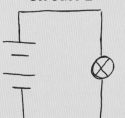

Will this circuit light the bulb? Explain your answer.

Circuit 3
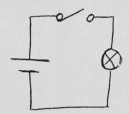

Will this circuit light the bulb? Explain your answer.

Circuit 4
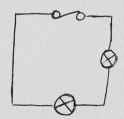

How many bulbs will light in this circuit? Explain your answer.

Circuit 5
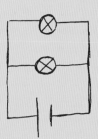

What is this kind of circuit called?

Circuit 6
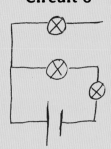

How many bulbs will light up in this circuit? Explain your answer.

Circuit 7
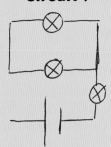

How many bulbs will light up in this circuit? Explain your answer.

Circuit 8
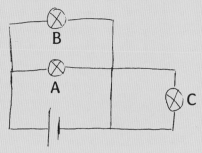

Where would you break the circuit so that only bulbs A and B will light up? How about to make only bulbs A and C light up?

Let's Talk!

What are the particles called that make up electric current?

Is a battery-powered toy an electrical item? Explain your answer.

Which would make a bulb shine brighter — a 9-volt battery or six 1.5-volt cells? Explain your answer.

Why is the switch in a circuit like a bridge connecting two roads?

You can download more activities and all the answers for pages 16 and 17.

Your Electricity's Journey

Mains electricity is produced in power stations. Like a battery, the power station pushes the electricity off around a giant circuit to your home and back again.

From a power station, electricity flows through underground cables or along high-voltage overhead lines strung between pylons.

Once the electricity is close to where it is needed, it flows through a substation. Then it continues its journey through more wires directly into your home.

When we switch on a light, the dishwasher or the TV, electricity is instantly there, flowing through the network of wires inside our homes.

High-Voltage Giants

There are about 88,000 electricity pylons in the UK. These tall steel towers support power lines that carry up to 400,000 volts of electricity.

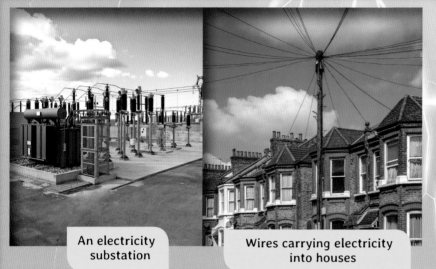

An electricity substation

Wires carrying electricity into houses

What Happens at a Substation?

At a substation, the voltage of the electricity is reduced. Electricity that's heading to a large factory might be reduced to about 33,000 volts. In the UK, the electricity that flows into our homes is reduced to 230 volts.

How Much Electricity?

Inside a home, shop or other building, electricity flows through a meter. This device calculates how much electricity has been used so people can pay their electricity supplier. Many people have smart meters that allow them to see how much electricity they are using in a day or even by the hour.

A smart meter

The National Grid

In the UK, the National Grid is a company that takes care of the electricity supply. Day and night, highly trained workers are on duty to make sure that enough electricity is going from power stations to homes, work places, hospitals, street lights – anywhere it is needed. For example, each morning at around 9 a.m., more power is needed as millions of people switch on computers and other machines to start work!

The National Grid takes care of the thousands of kilometres of power lines and cables that crisscross the country.

Power Stations

At power stations, different kinds of fuels, including natural gas, coal and oil, are used to **generate** electricity.

Generating Electricity

1. At a power station, fuel, such as gas or coal, is burned to boil water.

2. The boiling water produces steam.

3. The steam is used to turn giant, wheel-like machines called **turbines**.

4. The turbines turn a machine called a generator, which produces the electricity.

5. Next, the electricity goes through transformers. These devices increase its voltage up to 400,000 volts.

6. Finally, the electricity is ready to begin its journey through high-voltage lines and cables.

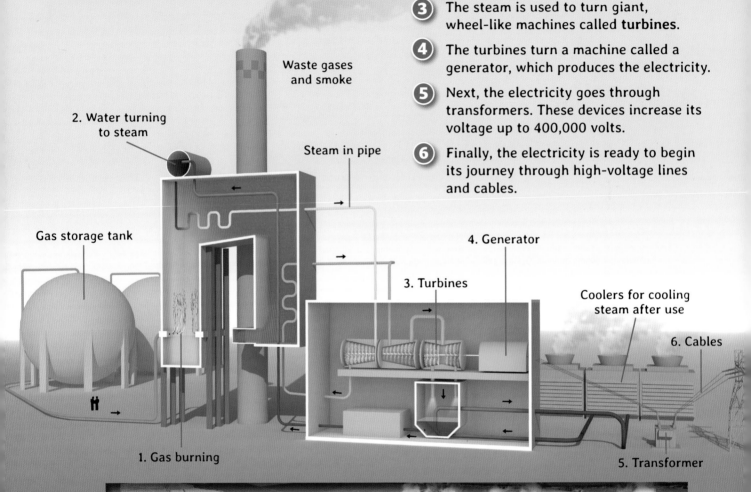

Waste gases and smoke

2. Water turning to steam

Steam in pipe

Gas storage tank

4. Generator

3. Turbines

Coolers for cooling steam after use

6. Cables

1. Gas burning

5. Transformer

The cooling towers release water vapour, a gas that forms when the hot water used to make steam is cooled down.

Drax power station in North Yorkshire, UK

Water vapour

Gas, coal and oil are called **fossil fuels.** They come from deep underground. Fossil fuels get this name because they formed millions of years ago in a process that's similar to how dinosaur fossils formed.

Coal

How Did Gas and Oil Form?

1. Sea plants and animals died and decayed (rotted) on the seabed.

2. Over millions of years, the remains were buried by layers of sand and soil. Heat and pressure turned them into oil and gas.

3. Today, we extract oil and gas from under the ground. It's transported to power stations on ships or through large pipes.

How Did Coal Form?

1. Plants died and settled on the bottoms of swamps, where they decayed (rotted).

2. Over millions of years, the plant remains were covered by layers of soil and water. Heat and pressure turned the plant remains into coal. In time, the water dried up.

3. Today, we mine (dig) the coal from underground. It is transported to power stations on trucks, trains and boats called barges.

Nuclear Power Stations

At a **nuclear power** station, a metal called uranium is used to make electricity. This is done by splitting the atoms of the uranium. Atoms are the tiny particles that make up everything in the universe, including you. As the uranium atoms split, they release a huge amount of heat energy which is then used to boil water to make steam. Then, just as in fossil fuel power stations, the steam turns the turbines that drive the electricity generators.

Renewable Electricity

In the UK, almost 70 percent of the electricity used comes from power stations that burn fossil fuels or produce electricity using nuclear power. But this isn't the only way to make electricity.

The ways in which countries around the world generate electricity can be grouped as **renewable** and **nonrenewable**.

Fossil fuels are **natural resources** that are nonrenewable. It took millions of years for them to form so we can't renew them, or make more.

We can, however, make electricity using the Sun, water power, wind, rubbish and even animal poo. These natural resources are renewable — they will never run out!

Crane operator

Electricity from Rubbish

At waste-to-energy power stations, rubbish from people's homes is the fuel instead of fossil fuels. Paper, cardboard, wood, garden cuttings and leftover food can all be burned to make electricity, instead of this rubbish going into **landfill**.

Rubbish in a storage bunker is picked up by cranes and dropped into the large, oven-like furnace for burning.

Poo Power

Animal dung and food waste can be put into a tank called a biodigester. As the mixture rots, it produces a gas called methane. This gas can be used to power a generator that produces electricity. In Toronto, Canada, poo from the animals at Toronto Zoo and out-of-date food waste from shops will be used to generate renewable electricity that will power local homes and businesses.

Elephant dung

Solar Power

Energy from the Sun can be used to make electricity. A solar panel is made up of lots of parts called solar cells. When sunlight hits the cells, the Sun's energy makes the electrons inside start to flow along the wires in the solar panel, creating electricity. If a person has solar panels on their roof, this electricity can flow straight into the wires inside their house.

In the UK, more than 30 percent of the electricity used comes from renewable resources and this is increasing each year!

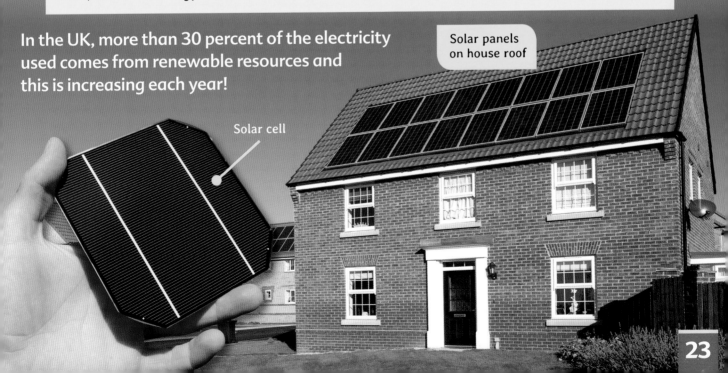

Solar panels on house roof

Solar cell

Wind and Water Power

When you turn on a tap, you can feel the power of water as it rushes over your hands. When the wind blows, you can feel its energy. Water and wind can both be used to generate electricity.

Wind turbines are giant windmills that can generate electricity. They are built on land and out in the ocean.

Water Power

At a hydroelectric power station, water in a river builds up behind a dam and forms a lake, or reservoir. When the water is released through the dam, it rushes past the turbines, making them spin. The spinning turbines turn a generator that makes electricity.

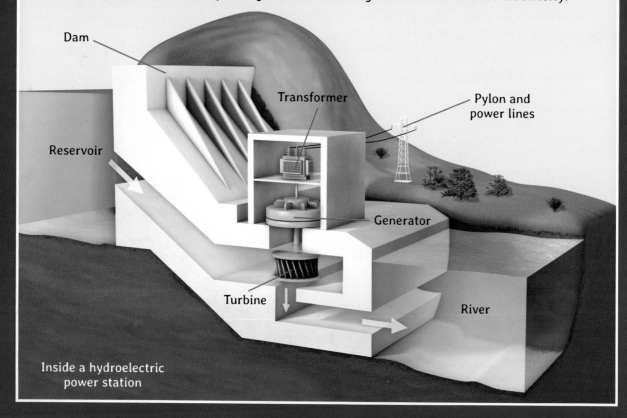

Dam

Transformer

Pylon and power lines

Reservoir

Generator

Turbine

River

Inside a hydroelectric power station

Inside a Wind Turbine

At the top of a wind turbine are three huge blades and a structure called a nacelle, which contains the turbine's generator.

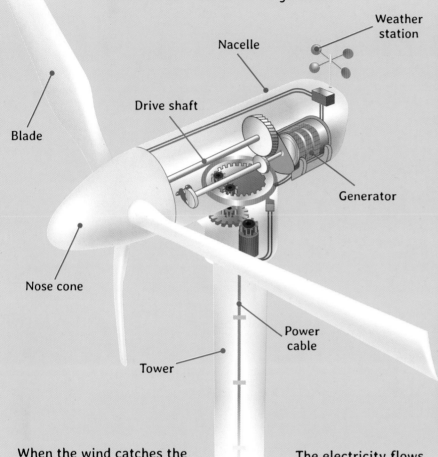

Weather station

Nacelle

Drive shaft

Blade

Generator

Nose cone

Power cable

Tower

When the wind catches the blades, they start to spin, turning a drive shaft. The drive shaft spins the generator, which produces electricity.

The electricity flows down a power cable inside the tower. Then the cable carries the electricity underground to wherever it is needed.

Catching the Wind

The weather station monitors the wind's speed and direction. It sends this information to the turbine's computer, which then turns the nacelle so the blades are always facing into the wind to capture the most energy.

Electricity and Climate Change

When fossil fuels are burned to make electricity, gases such as carbon dioxide, methane and nitrous oxide are released into the air. These gases are known as **greenhouse gases**.

The gases build up in Earth's **atmosphere** and trap too much heat from the Sun on Earth – just as a greenhouse traps heat. Many scientists believe that this is leading to a gradual increase in Earth's temperatures.

We need heat on Earth, but too much will be harmful. This change in Earth's temperatures is known as **climate change**. Making electricity with renewable energy sources, such as the Sun, wind and water, creates fewer greenhouse gases.

Meet the Wind Turbine Technicians

Imagine going to work by boat and then spending the day at the top of a tower that's more than 100 metres above the sea. It's all in a day's work for a wind turbine technician.

For the technicians who work at the Walney Offshore Wind Farm in the Irish Sea, the day begins at their control centre. They learn what tasks need to be carried out. Then they gather the equipment they will need.

Next, it's onto the boat for the hour-long journey out to the wind farm.

Blade

Nacelle

Ready for the Day

A turbine technician's equipment includes a laptop, tools and a climbing harness, a little like the ones rock climbers use. They also need a protective helmet and at cold times of year, a waterproof immersion suit to protect them from freezing water if they accidentally fall from the boat or tower. The technicians must also take lunch – there are no shops or cafes to visit when you're working at an offshore wind farm.

The technicians climb from the boat and up a ladder, being sure to attach themselves to the tower with their safety harnesses.

A boat carrying technicians arrives at a wind turbine

The team stops the turbine turning, and then they ride up to the nacelle in a tiny lift.

A day's work might include giving a turbine a service — just like the service that cars get. Parts are replaced and oiled. And any bits of broken machinery are fixed or replaced.

When all the work is done, it's back on the boat for the journey home.

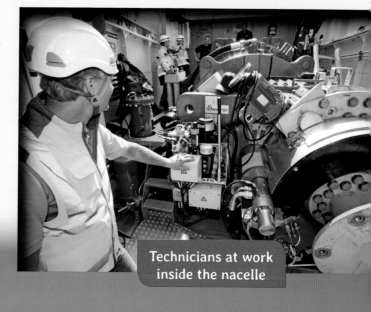

Technicians at work inside the nacelle

Turbine technicians might have to crawl around in tiny spaces. They may even have to climb inside the giant blades, or use ropes to make repairs to the outside of a blade!

Best and Worst

Technicians say that the best thing about their job is the fantastic view stretching for kilometres out to sea from the tops of the turbine towers. One of the worst things is that there are no toilets on a wind turbine. If you need to go, you have to get all the way back down to the boat to use the onboard toilet.

The Walney Offshore Wind Farm turbines produce enough electricity to power 600,000 homes.

Electricity in Our World

Cars that run on petrol or diesel produce greenhouse gases and other polluting fumes. Today, many people are choosing to switch to more environmentally friendly electric cars.

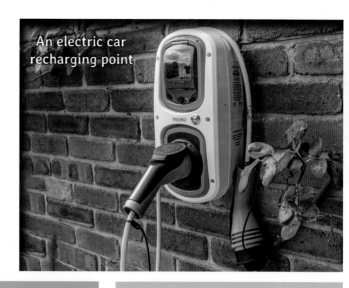
An electric car recharging point

An electric car's battery can be recharged by plugging the car into the electricity supply at the owner's home.

Charging stations for electric cars are appearing at the kerb on streets, at motorway service areas, fast food restaurants, supermarkets and places of work.

Recharging stations at a motorway service area

How "Green" Are Electric Cars?

The answer to this question depends on how the electricity is made. In the UK, a lot of electricity is still produced using fossil fuels. But as more and more electricity is produced using renewable methods, such as wind or solar, electric cars will become "greener". Also, unlike cars that burn petrol or diesel, electric cars do not produce polluting fumes.

Green Super Powers

The electric Tesla Roadster will be the fastest production car in the world in 2020. A production car is a vehicle that's designed to drive on roads, not on a racetrack. The Tesla Roadster can go from 0 to 100 km/h in just a couple of seconds, travel at up to 400 km/h and drive for more than 1000 kilometres on one recharge!

A Tesla Roadster

There's one kind of powerful electricity that lights up the whole sky — **lightning!**

Let's Talk!

How Lightning Forms

Lighting happens inside a giant thunderstorm cloud. The cloud gets so high in the sky that the air around it is very cold. Tiny crystals of ice form and mix with the water droplets that make up the cloud. Inside the cloud, the ice crystals move around, crashing into each other and creating electricity. The amount of electricity grows and grows until it creates a giant spark, or bolt of lightning!

In what ways have you used electricity today? Which of those tasks or activities would be impossible without the power of electricity?

About three-quarters of all lightning stays within clouds. About one-quarter hits the ground or objects such as trees or tall buildings.

A bolt of lightning heats the air around it to about 30,000°C.

Glossary

appliance
A piece of equipment that does a particular job — for example, a washing machine.

atmosphere
A layer of gases surrounding a planet, moon or star.

atoms
Tiny particles that make up everything around us.

battery
Two or more cells in which a chemical reaction takes place that creates electrical energy. In our everyday speech, a single cell may also be referred to as a battery.

cell
A device that can produce electrical energy. Two or more cells are known as a battery.

chemical reaction
A change that takes place between two or more substances and creates something new.

circuit
An unbroken loop or pathway of wire carrying electricity from a power source, such as a battery.

climate change
A gradual change in temperatures on Earth — for example, the current warming of temperatures caused by a build-up of greenhouse gases in the atmosphere.

component
A part of something — for example, a battery is a component of an electrical circuit.

conductor
A material that conducts electricity (or allows electricity to travel through it) — for example, copper.

electric current
A flow of electrons through a wire.

electron
A tiny particle that is part of an atom. Atoms are the particles that make up everything around us.

energy
The force that allows things to move and happen. There are different types of energy, such as electrical energy and light energy.

fossil fuels
Fuels that formed over millions of years from the remains of plants and animals. Oil, coal and natural gas are all fossil fuels.

generate
To produce or create.

greenhouse gases
Gases such as carbon dioxide, methane and nitrous oxide that occur naturally and are also released into Earth's atmosphere when fossil fuels are burned.

insulator
A material that does not conduct electricity — for example, plastic.

landfill
A place where a large quantity of rubbish is buried in the ground to get rid of it.

mains electricity
Electricity that is available through plugs in homes and other buildings.

materials
What things are made of — for example, copper and plastic are materials.

natural resource
Something that people use that is found in nature — for example, water and plants.

nonrenewable
A resource, such as coal, that cannot be replaced at the same rate as it is being used up.

nuclear power
A type of electricity. It is made by splitting uranium atoms and using the heat that is generated to make steam to run the turbines in a nuclear power station.

particle
A tiny part of something.

plug
A device that connects an appliance to mains electricity by *plugging* it into a socket.

power station
Large, factory-like buildings where electricity is generated.

pylon
A steel tower that supports the power lines that carry electricity.

renewable
A resource, such as the wind, that will not run out.

socket
A device that connects wires in a wall to a plug.

substation
A place where the voltage of electricity in power lines is reduced before it is delivered to homes and other buildings.

turbine
A wheel-like machine that turns and generates power. A turbine can be driven by steam, water or wind.

volt
A unit of measurement that measures voltage.

voltage
The push that causes electrical current to move in a wire or other electrical conductor.

Index

Answers

Page 5:
The vacuum cleaner and washing machine both plug into the electrical supply of a house. The electric toothbrush and phone are also powered by electricity. They have a battery inside, which is recharged by an electric-powered charger. The garden light works on electricity produced by its solar panel. The digital alarm clock is powered by a small battery which produces electrical energy. This type of lawnmower is powered by a person pushing. The kettle has no power source inside. The water inside is being heated by the gas burner. The alarm clock (wind-up) and barbecue (burning charcoal) do not use electricity.